This book belongs to

_____

This book is dedicated to my children - Mikey, Kobe, and Jojo.
Being brave means getting out of your comfort zone. Try to do one
brave thing a day.

Brave Ninja

By Mary Nhin

Pictures by
Jelena Stupar

"Oooh... ahhhh," exclaimed the crowd.

Brave Ninja was known to perform the best dives. It took a lot of courage to do those dives. That's why he was known to be the bravest ninja in the world.

When he was scared to do something, he summoned the courage to be brave.

When he was feeling worried, he visualized that all would be okay.

And when he felt anxious, he relaxed by taking a few deep breaths.

Brave Ninja wasn't always this courageous.

If he had to leave his parents for some time, he worried that something might happen to him or his parents.

Sometimes at night, he would be scared of things in the dark.

And if he was learning something new, he feared he would get hurt.

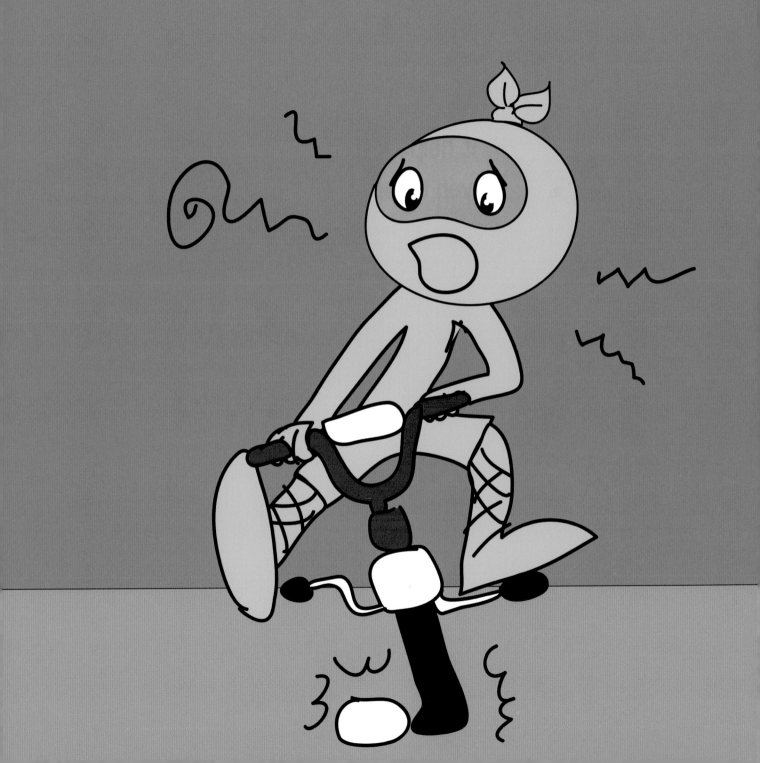

But things changed when Calm Ninja introduced
a strategy to help him be brave.

As Brave Ninja walked onto the diving board, he felt his heart beat faster, his hands shake, and his breath become quicker.

He took a few deep breaths and relaxed his muscles.

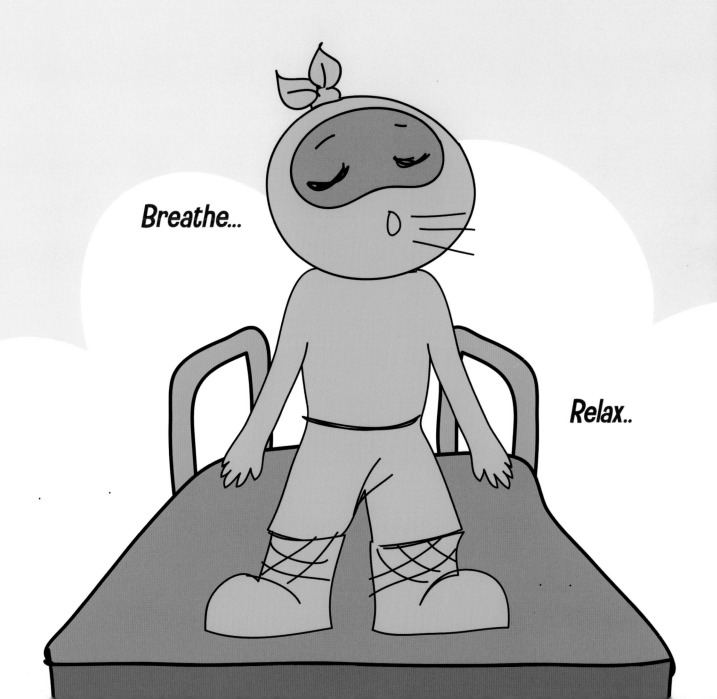

He smiled to show some positive body language. Then, he closed his eyes and visualized himself diving in.

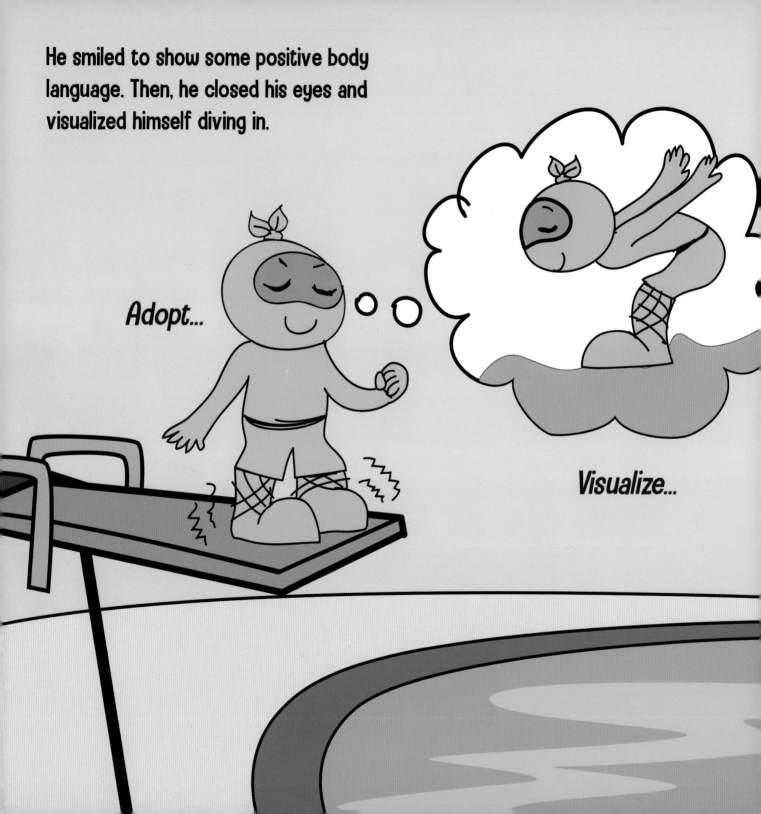

Adopt...

Visualize...

Much to his surprise, Brave Ninja survived. He *popped* up out of the water, beaming with pride.

BRAVE NINJA'S CHANT

When I don't feel brave,

I can remember that
being brave is a choice,

that I get to make with my
breath, body, and voice.

If you're ever feeling like you might need a little courage, remembering the B-R-A-V-E method could be your secret weapon against fear.

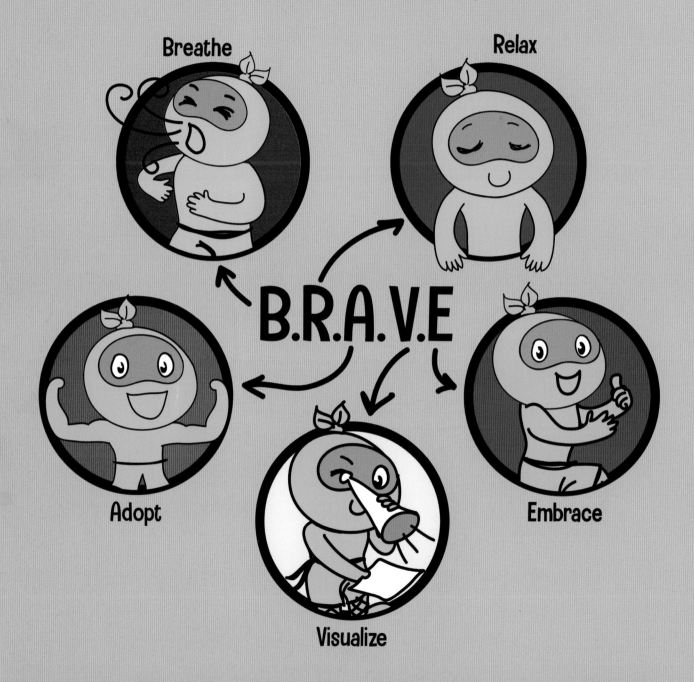

Breathe

Relax

B.R.A.V.E

Adopt

Visualize

Embrace

For free, fun printables, visit growgrit.co